Writing with a Purpose

Jean L. Pottle

J. WESTON
WALCH
PUBLISHER
Portland, Maine

1 2 3 4 5 6 7 8 9 10
ISBN 0-8251-3090-5

J. Weston Walch, Publisher
P.O. Box 658 • Portland, Maine 04104-0658

Printed in the United States of America

In memory of

two women who made a difference to me,

Winifred Carroll Pottle

and

Addie Violette Lemieux Wentworth

Contents

Overview

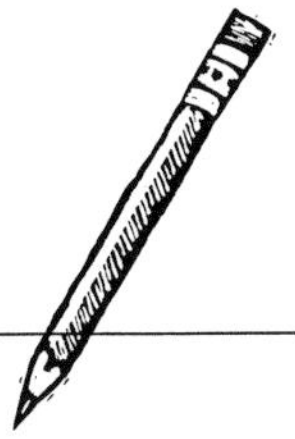

For the purposes of this book, there are four types of writing: informative, narrative, persuasive, and descriptive. Although it is extremely difficult to teach a formula for good writing, it is possible to show you that there are steps you can take to improve your writing whether your purpose is to inform, to describe, to tell a story, or to persuade. It is this book's goal to give you practice in following these steps.

The book is divided into four sections, one for each of the four writing types. Within each section, you first read a description of the writing type to be studied, followed by an example of this type of writing, as well as an outline of the example. This sequence enables you to see that a writing plan pulls thoughts and words together into a coherent pattern.

You have an opportunity to write about seven topics in each of the four sections of the book. Each section contains seven lessons. Each lesson provides you with background paragraphs, suggestions for topic sentences, and examples of how these sentences can be developed.

One writing subject, "Comfort Foods," remains constant throughout the four sections. The culminating activity in the book is to merge these four "Comfort Foods" pieces into a report on that subject. In this way, you are shown how to extend your writing beyond simple paragraphs.

Although each lesson can stand alone, it is probably more effective to read the introduction to a section and then complete at least two lessons in this section before moving on to another type of writing.

Throughout the book, you are reminded that your first drafts of assignments are rough drafts. Your teacher may ask you to write *all* your work in final draft form; or your teacher may ask you to select several pieces to revise, correct, and rewrite in final draft form.

Each section ends with "Revising and Editing Practice," which offers you an opportunity to revise and edit short pieces written by other students. You can find keys for these practice pieces at the end of this book. A glossary of terms used in the book is located on page *viii*.

Glossary

Con
an argument against a stated opinion

Developing a paragraph
supporting and expanding on the topic sentence

Editing
a two-step process of revising and proofreading for errors

Final copy
a finished piece of writing that has been edited

Grammar
following the accepted rules of language and punctuation

Pro
an argument in support of a stated opinion

Revising
rewriting and reorganizing a piece of writing

Rough draft
a piece of writing that has not been edited

Proofreading
reading a piece of writing for the purpose of correcting errors

Thesis
a stated opinion that the writer must support with persuasive evidence

Topic sentence
a sentence that presents the idea to be discussed in a paragraph

Transitional sentence
a sentence that connects one paragraph to another and transports or moves the reader on to the writer's next thought

Transitional word
a word that connects sentences or phrases

Informative Writing

I. Informative Writing

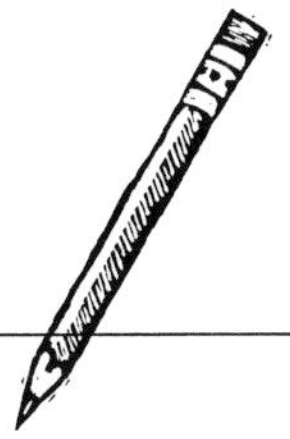

This type of writing provides information to the reader. It is sometimes called *expository writing* because its purpose is to "expose" facts. In order to be effective, informative writing should present clear information in a logical manner. Paragraphs should be introduced with strong sentences in which the writer states the purpose of the paragraphs. These sentences are called *topic sentences*.

Model Paragraph

It is important to write well. First, good writing allows you to express your ideas in such a way that others can understand what you mean. Second, when you express your ideas well, people pay attention to what you are saying. Third, good writing makes it possible for you to communicate with others inexpensively. Long-distance telephone calls are not necessary when what you want to say can be communicated for the price of a postage stamp. Lastly, good writing is permanent. What you speak is often lost as soon as the words leave your mouth, while what you write can be passed along for many generations. Think of it! Many people spend much of their lives studying the writing of people who lived hundreds of years ago.

Analysis of Model Paragraph

Notice how the writer developed the topic sentence with specific reasons.

It is important to write well.

1. Good writing is understandable.
2. People will read it attentively.
3. It is inexpensive communication.
4. It is permanent.

Before you begin writing an informative paragraph, it is important to stop and think about specific details that will support your ideas. Each lesson in this book has a brief introduction that is followed by a suggested topic sentence and paragraph pattern. In the first seven lessons, you will have an opportunity to practice writing informatively. Good luck.

1. Making Decisions

Each of us makes several decisions unconsciously every day of our life. Some are as simple as what kind of breakfast cereal we want, or how much time we can allow for eating that breakfast. It gets a little more complicated when we consider what we want to wear for a day away from home, and even more complicated when we are asked to meet some kind of deadline or to consider what type of work we would like to do for the rest of our lives.

For some people, decision making is easy. They just consider the question, whatever it is, make a decision, and then move on. Others consider options only to change their minds several times. These people frequently doubt the correctness of their decisions even after they have made them.

Which type of person are you? Your first writing assignment is to write an informative paragraph about making decisions. You may choose to use the topic sentence and details suggested, or you may develop your own.

Topic Sentence and Paragraph Pattern

For some of my friends, making decisions seems to be easy, but for me it is difficult.

1. Explain how a friend approaches decision making.
2. Give one specific example of a friend's decision.
3. Explain why you think this person decides so easily.
4. Finish the paragraph by writing one thing you could do to improve your decision-making process. Some people suggest making lists of the pros and cons of a decision. Others discuss decisions with friends or family before making a commitment. You must decide what works for you.

____

____

____

____

2. Evaluating a Comic Strip

Do you sometimes find yourself jumping to conclusions? That is, do you make up your mind that something is either good or bad without really thinking about why you are holding this point of view? Most of us are guilty of this at one time or another. Often we make snap decisions about the worth of an object or idea because we do not look beyond our initial reaction to it. In other words, we don't take the time to make an evaluation. To *evaluate* means to look at the strengths and weaknesses of something before making up our minds about it.

In this writing assignment, you are asked to evaluate a comic strip. Because the purpose of this piece of writing is to inform your reader, you must be sure that you include specific information to support your ideas. First, read the comic strip. Give it a + or – for its intent and effectiveness. Then look through the questions that follow it. These will help you to evaluate the strip fairly.

OK. You've read the strip. Answer the following questions about the strip.

1. Was its intent to be funny? ______________________________

2. Did you laugh at the end of the strip? ______________________

3. Why did you laugh? Was the artist depicting a common failing among people?

4. By looking at the first frame could you predict the last frame? Why? Why not?

5. Was any further information needed in order for the viewer to understand the strip?

6. Regardless of how you feel about the message the artist depicted, was the message clear? Why? Why not?

Topic Sentence and Paragraph Pattern

Before deciding whether a comic strip is good or bad, it is important to look at more than just the drawings.

1. Use your first reaction to the comic strip as an example of a quick judgment call.

2. Continue by explaining why you did or didn't laugh at the end of the strip. If you did laugh, you might describe a similar situation in which you played a part. If you didn't, explain why. Consider your answer to question 4 as you do this.

3. Finish up by using your answers to questions 4, 5, and 6 to support your evaluation of the worth of the strip. If you wish, you might go on to a separate paragraph in which you state how the strip could be improved.

3. A Life That Made a Difference ________

Of course, every life makes a difference. What you are asked to do in this writing assignment is to select an individual who you think has made a difference. Think about people you have read and heard about. You may even think about people you know.

Some notable people you might consider are Jackie Robinson, Duke Ellington, Harry Truman, Madame Curie, Marjory Stoneman Douglas, Margaret Chase Smith, Eleanor Roosevelt, Theodore Roosevelt, and the Beatles. There are hundreds more worthy of being considered. It's up to you to investigate who they might be.

Because the purpose of this piece is to inform your reader, you need to collect as much specific information as you can and then choose the information that will support your topic sentence. As in past assignments in this book, you do not need to use the topic sentence given. You may write your own.

Topic Sentence and Paragraph Pattern

______________________*'s life made a difference.*

1. Write a sentence in which you identify the person's accomplishment.
2. Continue by describing the difficulties this person faced in accomplishing this task.
3. Explain the difference that this accomplishment has made to you, to the community, to the country, to the world.
4. End your paragraph by referring back to your topic sentence in some way. You do not need to repeat it exactly. Try to remind your reader of the purpose of your paragraph. You want to echo the thought of that first sentence.

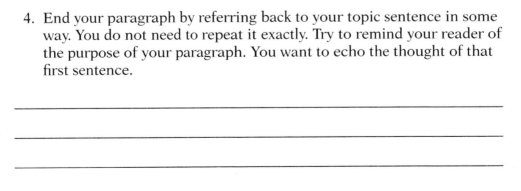

____

____

____

____

When you have followed these steps, you will have a strong rough draft.

4. Television Situation Comedies: Real Life? ___

How many situation comedies do you see each week? *Father Knows Best* was a favorite situation comedy way back in the 1950's. This was followed by such programs as *Ozzie and Harriet, The Munsters, Roseanne, Home Improvement,* and *Seinfeld.* Do you have a favorite? Have you ever stopped to think about why it is your favorite? Does the realism of the program make any difference to you?

What do you think the purpose of television comedies is? Is their purpose to depict real life? to entertain? to instruct? In this writing assignment you are asked to discuss the following question. Is it necessary for situation comedies to depict real life? This is a broad question and can cause problems for any writer.

One of the problems you may have is limiting your subject. First of all, there is no way that you can discuss all situation comedies in one paragraph. You must limit your topic. Furthermore, since this is an informative piece, you must base your work on facts. In order to do this, you need to limit yourself to one program. Not only that, within the framework of one paragraph, you must also limit yourself to considering only one element of the program. You might choose to concentrate on plot, characters, theme, or setting.

Before writing your paragraph, watch one episode of a program in which you are interested. Pay attention to only that specific element (plot, character, setting, theme) and take notes on that element only. Then, you are ready to write.

Topic Sentence and Paragraph Pattern

The purpose of this paragraph is to highlight the _______________ of one episode of ____.

1. In one sentence explain to the reader why you decided to select plot, character, theme, or setting.

2. Briefly describe the plot, characters, theme, or setting.

3. Complete your paragraph by asking your reader to decide whether what you have described is realistic. Do not include your opinion.

5. Trials and Tribulations of Being ________

So far, we have not discussed the advantages of writing more than one draft. Revising is to your advantage whenever you are developing a piece of writing for another person's consideration. Take the time to reread what you have written, revise awkward sentences, and if necessary, change the order of sentences so that your readers can understand the logic of your paragraph development. Having done all this, you then should check your spelling, grammar, and punctuation. After you have completed these two steps, revising and proofreading for errors, you are ready to write your final copy.

At first glance, the title of this writing assignment seems incomplete. That is because it is up to you to decide what trials and tribulations you are going to write about. The purpose of this writing assignment is to give you an opportunity to practice answering the kinds of questions you might be asked in many subject areas. Let's take as a beginning point the following: Describe the problems faced by an important contemporary or historical figure.

To begin with, you must identify a person and research information on that person. When that is done, you are ready to begin writing.

Topic Sentence and Paragraph Pattern

____________________ *faced a variety of trials and tribulations in his/her struggle to succeed.*

1. From your reading, select an obstacle this person had to face. You might begin this sentence by using the word "First." Explain how this person dealt with this first problem.

2. Name a second problem this person faced. Include the words "second problem" in your sentence. Again, take the time to explain this problem and how the person dealt with it.

3. Finish your paragraph by mentioning the success this person reached and by emphasizing that this was done in spite of the trials and tribulations that had to be faced and conquered. Be sure you mention the words "trials and tribulations," as they connect your answer to what you have been asked to do.

When you have finished your rough draft, reread your work and follow the suggestions in the first paragraph of this assignment before preparing your final copy.

6. The Road Not Taken

This is the title of a famous poem by Robert Frost, a twentieth-century New England poet. In this writing assignment you are going to practice an approach to answering a type of question frequently asked by your English or language arts teachers. That is the type of question in which you are asked to respond to a short story, novel, poem, or play. Where do you begin with such an open request? What happens when many writers face this situation is that they do not provide specific information that ties their answers to what has been asked. So a good way to begin is to repeat words found in the original question.

Let's say that your instructor has asked you to read the opening stanza of Frost's four-stanza poem and react to it.

> Two roads diverged in a yellow wood,
> And sorry I could not travel both
> And be one traveler, long I stood
> And looked down one as far as I could
> To where it bent in the underbrush

When faced with a group of words like this, what do you do? One way is simply to write what you have read in your own words. What is Frost saying in this poem? Obviously, he is talking about taking a walk and trying to decide where to go. Don't be afraid of poems or what poets have to say. Just plunge in and read the words as you would any other group of words. Let's say you decide, then, to begin the paragraph by restating the question in your own words and then by going on to write the plot of the stanza.

Topic Sentence and Paragraph Pattern

What is meant by the opening stanza of "The Road Not Taken"?

1. In a sentence or two, write your explanation of what happens in the first stanza.
2. Follow this with a question or statement in which you suggest the poet might be referring to more than a path in the woods.
3. Consider what other types of paths people follow in life. Suggest one of these paths in your next sentence.
4. Finish the paragraph by returning to your topic sentence and adding a comment about what happens when you follow any path. Can you be sure of where it will take you? Can you always find your way back?

What you have done in this answer is to write specifically about the poem. Keep this in mind the next time you face this type of situation—always refer back to the source.

7. Comfort Foods

If you look up "comfort" in the dictionary, you will find that it means to ease or soothe or to make comfortable. Most of us know that certain foods make us feel good, and many of us turn to those foods when we are unhappy or a little sad. Comfort foods are important in many countries and cultures. Because this is such a large topic, you are going to have the opportunity to write about it in four different ways: informatively, narratively, persuasively, and descriptively.

In your first paragraph on comfort foods, your task is to supply information about comfort foods. That information is probably best gained by discussing comfort foods with a variety of people of different ages. Plan to talk with at least 10 people before you begin to write this piece. During your conversations, be sure to keep notes. Ask the people what their favorite comfort food is. Ask when they first tasted it. Ask them also to describe the circumstances in which they turn to this comfort food. When you have all this information, complete the paragraph pattern below.

Topic Sentence and Paragraph Pattern

Choices of comfort foods vary a great deal from one person to another.

1. Look through your notes. Select two comfort foods that are very dissimilar. Name the two foods, and go on to describe the persons who selected them. Do not name those persons.

2. Continue by saying how many people you interviewed and giving examples of what they said about their favorite comfort foods.

3. Finish by making a statement based on what you heard during your interviews about how widely people vary in the foods they choose for comfort.

____

____

____

____

You have now completed a strong rough draft. If you wish to write this in final draft form, your first step is to reread your material and make any necessary changes. When you have done that, proofread the piece for spelling, punctuation, and grammar errors.

You will be returning to the subject of comfort foods at the end of the next section.

Editing Practice I

Your last assignment in this section of the book is to revise and edit a paragraph written by another student. Before you begin your work, consider the following paragraph and the revisions and editing comments made by one reader. The writer of the following piece was asked to write a paragraph detailing exactly how to make a mini pizza.

Mighty Mini Pizza

Line 1 The popularity of pizza is amazing. Everywhere you

Line 2 look in communitys across the country, you will find

Line 3 pizza parlors. Why is pizza popular. Probably because

Line 4 it is quickly made delicious and dirties few dishes.

Line 5 People usually think of Italy when they think of pizza,

Line 6 but other countries have similar dishes. To make a mini

Line 7 pizza you need a pakage of English muffins, a jar of

Line 8 tomato sauce, and your favorite toppings. Cut the

Line 9 muffins in half, spread tomato sauce over each half, and

Line 10 sprinkle your favorite toppings over the sauce. Place

Line 11 the muffins on a baking dish and broil for two or three

Line 12 minutes.

Revising and Editing Comments

The assignment was to write about how to make a mini pizza. The writer went way beyond the subject by including several sentences that have nothing to do with the subject of the paragraph. At first glance, it would be possible to think the topic sentence was "The popularity of pizza is amazing." Of course, this is not correct because the writer goes on to talk about where you can find pizza parlors as well as where pizza comes from. The writer did not limit the topic to discussing a recipe for mini pizzas.

Grammatical and Spelling Error Corrections

1. Line 2, communit**ies**
2. Line 3, popular**?**
3. Line 4, made**,**
4. Line 4, delicious**,**
5. Line 5, pizza**,**
6. Line 7, pa**c**kage

Now it's your turn. Read the paragraph on the following page. Comment on the organization of the paragraph and then go on to correct spelling and grammatical errors.

Student Assignment

Write a paragraph on a famous person who played a part in the development of human flight. Make clear in your topic sentence why you selected this individual. Turn in your rough draft iafter you have edited the paragraph.

Student Paper

Orville Wright

Line 1 Wilbur Wright was born in 1850 which meant he was older

Line 2 then Orville. Milton Wright, there father was a minister

Line 3 and liked to invent. Wilbur built a machine to fold the

Line 4 church newspapers. The brothers became interestd in

Line 5 flight when Milton Wright gave the boys a toy helicopter.

Line 6 the brothers began working together on a newspaper the

Line 7 West Side News in 1889. Its interesting that the first

Line 8 machine they worked on was a bicycle. The brothers did

Line 9 research and tested over a hundred wings. Finally in 1903

Line 10 there plane Flyer left the ground.

Narrative Writing

II. Narrative Writing

The purpose of narrative writing is to tell a story. Sometimes you tell a story simply to do just that, tell a story. Frequently, telling a story is a good way of developing a subject introduced in a topic sentence. By telling a story, you can help your reader understand the point you are trying to make. For example, read the following paragraph. The topic sentence is italicized. Notice how the story that follows explains the topic sentence.

Model Paragraph

Sometimes people can be so mean. Last week I was all excited about a new outfit I had bought. I saved it for a special occasion, a movie date with a group of friends. We all met in front of the theater all bundled up against an icy wind. I could hardly wait to take off my coat so that everyone could see my new outfit. Well, I slipped out of my coat in the lobby of the theater. My four friends took a look at the outfit. Sue, Bruce, and Selma gave me approving looks, but Tiffany spoiled it by saying, "Another hand-me-down from your sister?" [I can't understand why she wanted to be so mean.]

Analysis of Model Paragraph

Notice that the writer developed the paragraph by listing events in the order in which they happened. This is typical of narrative writing.

People can be so mean.

1. New outfit
2. Special occasion
3. One friend spoiled it

In Section II of this book, you will be writing on a variety of topics that will give you an opportunity to tell stories. In some, you will be writing just to tell a story. In others, you will use a story to support an idea introduced in a topic sentence. Just as in the first section, Informative Writing, you will have paragraph patterns to help you along your way.

8. It Was a Dark and Stormy Night

"It was a dark and stormy night" has been used to begin any number of mystery stories. This time it is your turn to tell a story with a dark and stormy night as the setting.

Because it is easier to write about what you know, try to describe a dark and stormy night that you can remember. Think back to a night when the winds raged and the rain or snow pelted against the windows. How did it make you feel? Did the lights go out? Did you worry about the storm doing damage to your house, or did you think of it as an adventure? Looking back at the experience, what might have happened? Use your imagination to create a story based on experience. If this isn't possible, think about the kinds of things that can happen on a dark and stormy night.

The topic sentence and paragraph pattern that follow will get you started.

Topic Sentence and Paragraph Pattern

President Franklin Roosevelt once said, "We have nothing to fear but fear itself."

1. Explain what you were afraid of one dark and stormy night.

2. Describe the action of the storm. Use strong words which help the reader to feel as you felt.

3. Describe what happened and how you reacted. If you are not basing your story on an actual event, you may introduce a suspicious stranger or a strange noise. Of course, you may do that anyway if you wish to do so.

4. Finish up the paragraph by explaining why there was nothing to be afraid of. In this way, you will be returning to the quotation that began your paragraph.

If this paragraph is going to be evaluated, you will need to edit your work carefully. Remember, there are two steps to this process.

1. Read your material for organizational problems and awkward sentences.

2. Read your material for grammatical and spelling errors.

9. My First Job

For this writing assignment, you are asked to think back to your very first job. Yes, your very first. It may have been when you were only six or seven, when a relative or neighbor asked you to do something as simple as rake leaves, clean your room, pick up your clothes, or maybe even run an errand. Maybe your first job was one you created for yourself. Many people begin their working lives by selling newspapers, magazines, or lemonade. Can you remember the very first time you actually felt a sense of responsibility for a task? It is this sense of responsibility that you need to focus on in this assignment. How did you feel as you began your job? Were you afraid that you would fail, or did you feel very confident that you could do the job without any trouble? Of course, you may not have thought about failure or success as you concentrated on doing what you had to do.

Now that you are older and have had more experience, you can look back at that first job and think about what you learned from the experience. Maybe you were not conscious at that time of any learning taking place, but now you can see that it did have some effect on you.

The topic sentence and paragraph pattern that follow may be changed in any way you wish, or you may use them exactly as they are written.

Topic Sentence and Paragraph Pattern

My first job may not sound like a very important one, but it made a great deal of difference to me.

1. Describe your first job and identify who gave it to you.
2. Explain why you think you were given the job.
3. Write a sentence in which you tell how you began work.
4. Describe how you finished up your task.
5. Tell your reader how you felt when your job was done. Complete your paragraph by returning to the idea expressed in your topic sentence.

You have probably noticed the frequent suggestion that you end your paragraph by returning to the idea expressed in your topic sentence. Although you do not always need to do this, it is a good way to remind your reader of the main idea of your paragraph. Remember, the topic sentence expresses an idea, and the remainder of the paragraph supports that idea.

10. Making Mistakes

Do you remember the story about the boy who cried "wolf" when he was in no danger? Townspeople who came to his rescue warned him that one day, when he faced real danger, no one would believe him. Of course, that is exactly what happened. One day he was alone in the fields surrounding his village when he was confronted by a wolf. He cried "Wolf!" but people ignored his cries, thinking it was just another false alarm. The storyteller did not reveal the boy's fate, but it doesn't take much to imagine what happened.

That boy (let's call him Ralph) made his first mistake the first time he cried wolf when there was no wolf around. Ralph made his second mistake when he refused to listen to the townspeople's warnings. Some people, as you know, never learn from their mistakes.

In this writing assignment, you are to use the story of the boy who cried wolf as a model. Make Ralph a modern-day teenager who has a modern-day teenager's problems. Develop a situation in which he cries out for help when he really doesn't need it. It's up to you to decide what happens when he cries out because of real danger.

You may use the topic sentence and paragraph pattern that follow, or you may develop your own based on the Ralph-and-wolf idea.

Topic Sentence and Paragraph Pattern

Everyone makes mistakes, but not everyone learns from making those mistakes.

1. Describe the kind of person Ralph is.
2. Set the scene for his mistake.
3. Explain the reaction to his mistake.
4. What did Ralph do in response to this reaction?
5. What happened to Ralph?
6. Return to your topic sentence by commenting on learning from mistakes.

You may find that you want to extend this story beyond one paragraph. If you decide to do this, remember to introduce your second paragraph with a clear topic sentence.

11. Humpty Dumpty

Do you remember this rhyme?

> Humpty Dumpty sat on a wall.
> Humpty Dumpty had a great fall.
> All the King's horses and all the King's men
> Couldn't put Humpty Dumpty together again.

This rhyme, like many others we have heard throughout our lives, is repeated over and over, but no one ever seems to stop and think about why Humpty had his fall or why the King's horses and men tried to put him back together.

In this lesson, you are asked to devise a story that explains who Humpty Dumpty was and what kind of fall he had. Did he literally fall off a wall and break, or does his fall represent the loss of a job, an opportunity, or a public office of some type? You have a chance to make history by explaining who this strange person Humpty Dumpty was.

The topic sentence and paragraph pattern that follow may help to get you started. If you decide to go on to a second paragraph, be sure that the topic sentence that introduces the second paragraph makes clear to your reader what your paragraph will be about. Since this is narrative writing and you are creating a story, you can let your imagination run free.

Topic Sentence and Paragraph Pattern

My goal is to tell you the story of Humpty Dumpty, to whom history has been unfair.

1. Explain Humpty Dumpty's background, including place of birth, education, and career.
2. Describe the situation in which Humpty Dumpty found himself that caused his initial problem.
3. What was Humpty Dumpty's reaction to this problem?
4. What kind of fall did he take?
5. Why was he not able to recover from this fall?

6. Return to the idea of your topic sentence. Mention also the role you have played in defending Humpty Dumpty's good name.

If this is to be written as a final draft, don't forget to complete the two-step editing process.

12. Traditions

It is traditional in a family that I know to meet each Fourth of July at a lakeside camp, which has been owned by family members for more than 60 years. Not only does the entire family (including parents, grandparents, great-grandparents, aunts, uncles, and dozens of children) meet in the same spot each year, they also enjoy the same menu enjoyed by previous generations.

Not everyone, of course, has such a long-standing tradition. But most of us do look forward to a traditional meal, gathering, sports event, or trip. What is a tradition that has been established in your life? What is something that you do each year at a particular time?

In this lesson, you are asked to write about this tradition and why it is important to you. What does it mean to you? How would you feel if you were not able to participate in this traditional event?

As with all the lessons in this book, you are provided with a topic sentence and a paragraph pattern which you may follow. Feel free to deviate from them as you see fit. If you wish to write more than one paragraph, take care with your topic sentence.

Topic Sentence and Paragraph Pattern

I like surprises, but I must admit that it is nice to know that certain events are going to take place at certain times.

1. Name the traditional event you look forward to and mention when it takes place.
2. Explain what started this tradition.
3. Go on to describe what happens.
4. Finish the paragraph by explaining why this event is so important to you.

13. Responding to a Question

Often a teacher will ask that you explain your answer to a question by supporting it with an example. Storytelling works very well in this type of situation.

Let's say, for example, that you were asked to identify a historical figure in whom you were interested and to support your answer with reasons for your choice. Let's say that you selected Abraham Lincoln. You might begin your paragraph by first naming Lincoln and then telling a story about Lincoln that explains why you selected him.

I have always admired and been interested in Abraham Lincoln because he was a man determined to get things done. Lincoln started with little but managed to accomplish a great deal. The story is told that he loved reading so much that he would walk miles to borrow a book and then spend his evenings reading by the light of the fire. Imagine, he didn't even have candles to read by! Today we have electric lights, and kids make excuses for not reading and doing their homework. Lincoln didn't make excuses. When he set his mind on a goal, whether it was gaining knowledge or solving the problems of our country, he worked until the goal was reached.

For this lesson, you are to answer the following question about a person you admire and then support your answer with a story from that person's life.

The question: Who is someone you admire? Explain your choice.

Topic Sentence and Paragraph Pattern

What does a person have to do to gain the admiration of others?

1. Explain what character trait you find particularly admirable. It might be courage, humor, or concern for others. Describe that trait.
2. Tell a story in which the person you admire demonstrates that trait. Give specific details.
3. Go on to explain why you think this trait is so important.
4. End your paragraph by stating once again that you admire this individual.

14. Comfort Foods

In the first section of this book, you were given an opportunity to do a survey to discover what other people saw as comfort foods. Here, in the narrative section of the book, you are asked to describe your own favorite comfort food and to describe an event in which your comfort food played a part.

For example, there was a very famous food writer who once told the story of her comfort food. You would expect that this person would have selected a very special meal in a very special restaurant. This did not prove to be true. Instead, she described a day when she had been overwhelmed by one problem after another. Awaking in the middle of the night absolutely starving, she crept down the stairs, went to the section of her kitchen where she kept her canned goods, and selected a can of tomato soup, which she heated up in a pan with a little milk, salt, and pepper. She then poured the soup into a bowl and sat down in a rocking chair to spoon this warm, comfortable soup into her mouth.

Now it's your turn. First, try to think of a food that you particularly enjoy. Then try to remember a particular time when you enjoyed eating your special treat. This does not have to be an unusual event. It can just be an everyday event that you remember.

A suggested topic sentence and paragraph pattern follow.

Topic Sentence and Paragraph Pattern

When I've had a bad day or when I am upset about something, I like to take the time to enjoy one of my favorite comfort foods.

1. Name your favorite comfort food.
2. Explain how frequently you enjoy your special treat.
3. Describe a particular time you can remember when this treat made you feel good.
4. Explain why you think this food is so special.
5. End your paragraph by returning to the idea stated in your topic sentence.

If this is to become a final draft, remember your two-step editing process.

Editing Practice II

If you are doing these writing assignments out of sequence, now is a good time for you to look at the first editing assignment, on page 19 of this book. If that is not possible, just keep in mind that the following piece of writing has a variety of problems that are your job to correct. This of course is a rough draft, so your first job is to indicate what kinds of organizational problems exist, and what sentences should be revised for clarity. After you have done these two things, go on to make corrections in grammar and spelling. Remember that every writer needs encouragement. Make at least one positive comment about the story.

Notice the assignment that the student was given.

Student Assignment

Write a story in which you prove the old adage "You can't judge a book by its cover." Be sure that you arrange your story in chronological order. Begin your writing with a topic sentence that tells your reader why you are telling the story. When you are finished, reread your work and look for ways to improve your sentences. Do not worry about correcting spelling and punctuation until after you have revised the content.

Student Paper

Neighbors

Charlie Coombs had lived next to old Mrs. Harris for as long as he could remember and Mrs. Harris had always been kind of grouchy. She was especially angry when Charlie's baseballs went into her yard but usually she wouldn't return them and Charlie didn't much like her.

One afternoon Charlie and Maria were batting around a few baseballs when one sailed into old Mrs. Harris yard and Charlie said, "That's it." Charlie said. "We'll never see that one again.

Suddenly from the other side of the fence a voice

said, “Doesn’t anyone teach you kids how to hit a ball?” And to Charlie and Marias surprise, Mrs. Harris face appeared over the fence and she held up a baseball in one hand and a bat in the other. “Let me give you a few tips,” she said. “My boy and I used to play a lot of baseball before he died several years ago. I haven’t even watched a ball game in years, but its time I took you two in hand. Your pathetic.”

It was then that Charlie remembered his mother telling him that Mrs. Harris’ son had died from a rare disease the year before Charlie’s family had moved into there home.

Charlie wondered if it was the memory of her son that had made Mrs. Harris tough on kids and if that was why she had always been unfriendly.

Persuasive Writing

III. Persuasive Writing

Convincing people to agree or disagree with a particular position isn't always easy. Most people make up their minds about an issue and then are reluctant to change their thinking. In persuasive writing, you learn how to put your ideas together in such a logical way that people pay attention to your ideas. Notice the italicized topic sentence in the following example, and then try to identify the way in which the writer makes her point.

Model Paragraph

I know the expression, "The early bird gets the worm." But who cares? I'm not a bird and I don't like worms. *Getting up and beginning a new day should be a pleasure, not a chore.* Morning is a time to think about the possibilities of a new day, rather than rushing around getting all worn out before the sun has had a chance to rise. It is time, as nutritionists tell us, to eat a good breakfast, one that will stay with us for the rest of the day. Who can take the time for a good breakfast if it's rush, rush, rush? It's time we slowed down to enjoy a beautiful part of the day rather than scheduling ourselves in such a way that we forget to appreciate the possibilities that a new day offers us.

Analysis of Model Paragraph

The writer developed her piece by first disputing a familiar phrase having to do with getting up early. Notice that her topic sentence was not the first sentence in the paragraph. Sometimes it is more effective to begin a paragraph with a quotation or phrase and then move on to the topic sentence. Notice how the writer supports the idea of the importance of beginning each day in a positive manner.

Getting up and beginning a new day should be a pleasure, not a chore.

1. Early bird gets the worm.

2. I'm not a bird.

3. We need time to plan the day.

4. We need to eat a good breakfast.

5. Getting up should be a pleasure.

In this section, you will have an opportunity to write several persuasive pieces. Remember that to be convincing you must give sound reasons for your thinking. Be as specific as possible, and try to include details that are based on fact rather than emotion.

15. The Best Place to Live

In this writing assignment, you are asked to take a stand on whether the country or the city is the better place to live. It may be that you don't feel strongly about this issue, but put that aside for now. When doing this kind of writing, it is best to start out by doing some reading and thinking about the subject. Once you have a little background, you are ready to take a position and present supporting information to your reader. Because of the nature of this assignment, you may want to write more than one paragraph.

Before beginning this writing assignment, make a list of the pros and cons of living in the country. A couple of suggestions have already been made.

Country Life	
Pros +	**Cons –**
Quiet, peaceful	Nothing to do

City Life	
Pros +	**Cons –**
Lots of things to do	Noisy

Now you are ready to write. The blank lines in the following topic sentence give you a chance to fill in the word "city" or "country."

Topic Sentence and Paragraph Pattern

For a number of reasons, the ________________ *is a better place to live than the* ________________.

1. Follow your topic sentence with two or three general comments about life in the area you have chosen.

2. Look through your list of cons. Pick out the con that you think is most regularly used as a reason for not enjoying the city or country. Think of a fact or an argument that disproves this con. Begin your second paragraph with this con and then write your disproving argument.

3. Think of at least two pros for the city/country and support these pros with specific evidence. You may want to write each pro in a separate paragraph and follow the pro with support for this point.

4. Begin your last paragraph by returning to your topic sentence and briefly renaming your pros. It is always best to end a persuasive piece by reminding your reader of the reasons for your point of view.

16. Dress Codes

When a dress code is mentioned, most people immediately think of school dress codes, although it is not only schools that have dress codes. Think about it for a minute: Nurses usually wear uniforms; city bus drivers wear uniforms; most business executives wear suits; and until recently, most office workers were expected to dress more formally than they would if they were at home. Change is in the wind, however, as more and more businesses are allowing their workers to dress informally.

Still, in many communities the question of dress codes in schools is seriously debated. Some parents and teachers feel that general behavior is improved when students have minimum dress-code guidelines, if not uniforms.

What do you think about this issue? Would you be prepared to follow a dress code if one were established at your school? In some schools students are required to wear uniforms. Is this a good idea? Would it make school life a little easier if students were not concerned about having and wearing the latest styles?

In this writing assignment, you are asked to take a position either for or against dress codes. Before you begin, talk about this issue with your friends. Explore the resources available through your library or on the Internet. After you have a little more background on this issue, make a list of pros and cons.

The question: Should dress codes be established in schools?

Dress Codes	
Pros +	**Cons** –

Now you are ready to write. You may use the topic sentence and paragraph patterns that follow, or you may develop your own. Notice that the topic sentence has a blank line for you to insert either "good" or "bad," depending on your opinion. Notice also that in this assignment you will be writing more than one paragraph.

Topic Sentence and Paragraph Pattern

Expecting students to follow a dress code is a _________ idea for many reasons.

1. Continue this paragraph by naming your reasons for thinking as you do. Do not explain each reason. You will be doing that in the paragraphs that follow.
2. Now, think of the strongest reason people might have for not agreeing with you. Begin a second paragraph with this reason and follow it with evidence that proves this opinion is wrong. From here on, your paper will present the pros for your position.
3. Now, write a sentence stating one of your pros. Follow this with sentences in which you give support for your pro.
4. If possible, write one more pro and finish off the paragraph with support for this pro.
5. In your last paragraph, return to the ideas you expressed in your topic sentence. Restate your opinion, and once again list the reasons as you did in the first paragraph. Always leave your reader with your point of view in his/her mind.

17. Mandatory Seat Belts

How do you feel about wearing a seat belt? Should everyone in a vehicle wear one? Should countries enforce seat-belt laws, or should this be a decision that individuals make? Many people would cite safety as the reason for insisting that everyone in a moving vehicle be strapped in. Others would say that by forcing people to wear seat belts, we are depriving them of the freedom that the U.S Constitution allows.

Obviously, there are pros and cons to this issue. It is your job in this writing assignment to do some background reading and seriously consider the options. You may want to look for instances in which people either did or didn't wear seatbelts and what happened to them when they were in an accident. Remember that in a persuasive piece you must try to be objective. As you write this piece, step back and do not allow yourself to use the word "I." When you use "I," you are making your writing personal. In persuasive writing, it is best to gather such strong evidence that personal emotion does not enter the work.

Now it's time to list your pros and cons.

Mandatory Seat Belts	
Pros +	**Cons –**

As in previous lessons, a topic sentence and a sentence pattern are supplied.

Topic Sentence and Paragraph Pattern

For a number of reasons, passengers in a moving vehicle (should/should not) wear seat belts.

1. Follow your topic sentence with a description of an event in which seat belts played a part. Obviously, if you are for seat belts, you will describe an incident in which people were saved because they were wearing seatbelts. If you are opposed to seat belts, you need an incident where seat belts proved a hindrance.

2. Follow this paragraph with the strongest argument against your point of view. Once you have stated it, you must prove this argument false.

3. Now, write your reasons for thinking as you do.

4. In the last paragraph of your paper, repeat your point of view and finish with a strong sentence in which you state what will happen if people don't follow the advice you are giving.

18. The Great Whatever Campaign

The writing assignment that follows is a little different from others in this writing series. Here you are asked to pretend that you are an advertising executive who must convince people to buy a specific product. As you know, advertising is everywhere—in magazines, in newspapers, on television, in store windows and even on billboards in some areas. What makes an advertising campaign successful? Why does one product sell better than another?

In this assignment, you must first create a product. It can be anything from a new television adventure series to a new type of pizza or a new type of sneaker design. You must then list the advantages of this product over all others of its kind. Finally, you will write a news story in which you introduce this product to consumers.

Product: ______________________________

Description: ______________________________

____

Advantages over competitors: ______________________________

____

____

____

____

Now that you have some information to work with, you are ready to write a news story. A topic sentence and a paragraph pattern follow. Notice that a name has been supplied for the company producing the product. You do not have to use this name; feel free to create your own.

Topic Sentence and Paragraph Pattern

The Whatever Company of Wannabuy announces the development of a product that no one will want to be without.

1. In the next sentence, name the product and what it can do.
2. In your third sentence, describe the many benefits of your product.

3. Go on to explain the advantages of this product over others of its kind.
4. Tell when the product will be available and where.
5. If you wish to continue your news story, you might name the person who created the product and describe the situation in which the product was created.
6. Your last sentence should be a strongly worded sentence in which you assure consumers that this product is essential to their future happiness.

19. Setting Standards

Being able to express your opinions and support those opinions in a persuasive way will help you in a variety of situations. When presenting a persuasive argument, a writer usually gives some general background on the subject, including a clear statement of opinion. This statement is called a *thesis*. The purpose of the thesis is to state what the writer hopes the reader will believe after the paper has been read.

The writer often goes on to consider the arguments that might be made against the thesis and supplies information to prove that each of those arguments is false. The writer then moves on to give reasons for the reader to accept the thesis.

In the following assignment, you are asked to put yourself in the place of an English teacher who is trying to persuade her students that it is important to have writing standards for class work. As you can imagine, the students do not see the importance of taking pains with all the work that is required of them. It is up to you to write a paper in which you convince students that standards are important.

Topic Sentence and Paragraph Pattern

The quality of your written work reflects on you.

1. Explain that what is written down in black and white is what the reader has to judge. What the writer intended to say or do makes no difference.
2. Express the students' point of view that it is difficult to fuss with every single bit of work. You might begin such a sentence with "Some students might say . . ."
3. Present the argument you think a teacher might offer.
4. Go on to explain why setting standards is important in school work and later in life.
5. If you wish to give an example of a situation in which good work paid off, you could begin a new paragraph by saying, "The following example shows the advantages of doing good work."
6. You should end your piece by returning to your thesis.

20. Toothpaste Tube Dilemma

Sometimes people get into arguments over very small things. For example, have you ever heard people disagree on which end of the toothpaste tube should be squeezed in order to remove the toothpaste? Have you heard some people say that it makes absolutely no difference, while others maintain that if the tube is squeezed from the top, toothpaste is wasted, or that if it is squeezed from the middle, the result is a messy tube? The arguments go on, and seldom is the issue resolved.

In this writing assignment, you are asked to take a rather "superior" attitude. Decide which part of the tube you think should be squeezed, and then defend your position with the best arguments you can summon. Although this assignment is meant to be fun, you will organize your material the same way you organized it in earlier persuasive pieces. Remember to list pros and cons before you begin writing.

You may use the topic sentence and paragraph pattern below, or you may create your own.

Topic Sentence and Paragraph Pattern

Toothpaste tubes were designed to be squeezed from the ___________.

1. Describe what happens when another procedure is followed.
2. Go on to deal with the strongest argument you think might be used against your position.
3. Give two strong reasons why your position is the better of the two. Supply evidence to support each reason. You may wish to do this by writing a separate paragraph for each reason.
4. Finish your piece by returning to your thesis statement and once again listing your reasons in slightly different words from those which you used earlier in your paper.

___

___

___

21. Comfort Foods ____________________

In a previous assignment, you wrote an informative piece about comfort foods in which you surveyed other people's preferences. In your second comfort foods assignment, you told a story about an occasion in which you enjoyed one of the foods from which you get pleasure and comfort. In this section, you are asked to write persuasively about a comfort food you think others should enjoy.

If you can't think of a comfort food that you feel strongly about, select a food that many people do not like. Broccoli, carrots, and spinach are frequently eyed with a lack of enthusiasm. Do you like them? One of them might be ideal for this assignment. What you must do is think of all the reasons for eating such food and consider what it is about the food that people dislike. For example, some people claim spinach is "slimy." Remember, you must be logical and persuasive. The blank line at the beginning of the topic sentence gives you an opportunity to fit in the food you have chosen.

Topic Sentence and Paragraph Pattern

_______________ *is a food which should be part of everyone's diet because of its many health benefits and because of the variety of ways it can be prepared.*

1. In the next sentence, explain why you think some people do not like the food you have selected.
2. Explain why this criticism is not valid.
3. Describe the benefits of eating this food. You might want to write about two benefits and give each benefit its own paragraph. Your topic sentence for these paragraphs might begin, "One of the benefits of eating _______________ is . . ." Be sure that you support your topic sentences with examples, description, or a brief story.
4. Because you mentioned in your topic sentence that this food can be prepared in a variety of ways, you need to write a sentence or two explaining a couple of ways in which the food may be prepared. For example, spinach can be steamed and served with a little butter and salt and pepper. It can also be eaten as one of the layers in a lasagna.
5. Finish up your piece by returning to the thesis you wrote about in your topic sentence. Try to end with a familiar saying that applies to what you have written. For example, "Remember, you are what you eat."

Editing Practice III

Read the following essay and suggest ways in which the writer could improve this piece. Look first at the instructions to be sure that the writer has completed the work as assigned. Then move on to organization. Has the writer written clear topic sentences for each paragraph? Is each topic sentence supported by specific information? When this is done, move on to make positive comments on the piece. Show that you recognize the strengths of the writing. Lastly, check for grammar, punctuation, and spelling errors.

Student Assignment

Write a 500-word essay in which you support the topic sentence "The Latin language is alive and well." Introduce your subject, suggest an argument against this statement (your thesis), show how this argument is false, offer a pro for your thesis, and support it with a well-developed paragraph. Write another pro for your thesis with good supporting evidence. Finish the paper by returning to your thesis statement.

Student Paper

If Latin Isn't Dead, It Must Be Alive

Line 1 Students first learning latin like to repeat this

Line 2 jingle:

Line 3 Latin is a language as dead as it can be.

Line 4 First it killed the romans;

Line 5 Now it's killing me.

Line 6 While its true that learning Latin requires real effort,

Line 7 Latin is hardly a "dead" language. Latin is alive and

Line 8 well.

Line 9 The obvious response to the claim that Latin is a dead

Line 10 language is that any language that is not spoken

Line 11 somewhere in the world by some group of people cannot be

Line 12 considered anything but a dead language. True, no group of people speaks latin per se, but more than half know Latin morphemes are still used everyday as English words. This certainly is not a description of a dead language.

Latin lives through some of our most treasured American Documents. The Preamble to the Constitution of the United States, for example, contains more then 20 words that have Latin roots.

In addition, Latin lives through the many students who have learned to appreciate the structure of the English language through their study of Latin. Because of Latin's precise grammatical relationships, students who study the language are able to transfer what they have learned about Latin to their understanding of the structure of the english language.

The Latin language is alive and well because every English-speaking person is knowingly or unknowingly keeping it from dying by reading historical documents, by conversing with friends, and by writing essays. Each one of us is a defender of the language. Keep up the good fight!

Descriptive Writing

IV. Descriptive Writing

People often think of descriptive writing as painting a picture with words. Descriptive writing can appeal to much more than the sense of sight. The writing can appeal to the reader's sense of touch, smell, hearing, and even taste. Descriptive writing can stand on its own, or it may be used to develop a topic sentence, as it was in the following example.

Model Paragraph

It was a desolate sight. What had once been a beautiful Victorian home with wide windows and comfortable looking porches was now merely a blackened shell. Smoldering debris sent clouds of sooty smoke into the starless night sky. The occasional snap of fire, not yet through with its destructive work, kept onlookers alert as an icy wind swept through the remains of what had once been a thing of beauty and comfort.

Analysis of Model Paragraph

The writer developed this paragraph by supplying descriptive words to help the reader hear, see, feel, and smell the fire scene.

It was a desolate sight.

1. It had been a comfortable home.
2. Now a blackened shell
3. Smoldering debris
4. Snap of fire
5. Icy wind

In this section, you will write several descriptive pieces, using descriptive details to expand topic sentences. Don't forget to edit any draft that is to become a final draft.

22. The Stranger

Your first assignment in the descriptive section of *Writing with a Purpose* is one in which you will have to stretch your imagination. Throughout your lifetime, you have seen hundreds of strangers. You have seen them on the streets of your town or city, observed them in crowds on television, and noticed them at ball games or other events. You may find that you are unable to write a description of any one of these people because you can't remember exactly what any of them looked like. If that is true, you will have to imagine a stranger to describe.

First, you need to know the setting in which you are to imagine this stranger. Are you ready?

The Setting

It is a rainy, dark September evening. The wind is dashing the rain against the windows of your house. There is a knock at the door. You jump to your feet and race to the door. When you open it you see . . .

The Stranger

1. Male, female, age?
   Suggestions: Older man, young woman, elderly female are possibilities. Think of your own.

___

2. Height and weight?
   Suggestions: Tall and slender, thin and stooped, short and roly-poly are possibilities. Now add your own.

___

3. Hair and eyes?
   Suggestions: Squinting eyes, carefully waved hair, and balding are some suggestions. Now add your own.

___

4. Type of clothing
   Suggestions: Dressed in torn jeans, wearing ropes of bright jewels, clothed in black are some possibilities. Think of your own.

___

5. Distinctive characteristics
   Suggestions: Mole on cheek, hooked nose, bright smile are some possibilities. Add your own words on the line below.

___

6. Manner
   Suggestions: Friendly, menacing, fearful are some possibilities. Add your own.

___

Now you are ready to write your description. A topic sentence and a paragraph pattern are supplied to get you started. Don't hesitate to make any changes that you feel are necessary.

Topic Sentence and Paragraph Pattern

When I opened the door of my house on that dark and rainy evening in September, I was confronted by a stranger.

1. Describe the stranger, using the words you have listed.
2. Based on the type of words you have used, write the reason the stranger had for knocking on your door.
3. Briefly explain your reaction.
4. End with a sentence in which your tell your reader why you reacted that way.

___

___

___

___

___

23. Night Sounds

How often do you really listen to the sounds around you? Most of us don't hear these sounds unless we are alone and there is nothing to distract us from what is going on around us. Stop for just a minute now to listen. On the lines below, make a list of the sounds that you can hear. Be sure to listen beyond voices.

Were you surprised at what you could hear? Remember, when you are really trying to hear, you must focus on sound alone.

In this assignment, you are asked to use your listening skills at night rather than in the daytime. The reason for this is that at night the world seems to quiet down a bit, and noises we would overlook in the rush of daily life are suddenly clear.

To prepare for doing this assignment, you will need a quiet room or a quiet spot outside. Sit down with pencil and paper and make a list of all that you hear. You may not be able to name every sound that you hear. At least try to describe the sound that the unknown insect, bird, machine, or person is making. When you have completed your list, you will be ready to follow the topic sentence and paragraph pattern that follow. Remember, in descriptive writing, you are trying to help your reader see, hear, touch, taste, and smell what you are describing.

Topic Sentence and Paragraph Pattern

If you think that it is quieter at night than it is in the daytime, you need to spend some time listening to night sounds.

1. Describe the time and the location of your listening experience.

2. Name the loudest sound that you heard, and try to duplicate the sound through nonword letter combinations. For example, the sound of an insect might be "buzz."

3. Go on to mention any other sounds that you heard. If you heard any sounds that made you feel uncomfortable, say so.

4. Were you aware of your own heart beating or the sound of your own breathing? If so, you might begin a sentence, "It was so quiet that I could hear . . ."

5. Finish your paragraph by making a general comment about night sounds. Try to tie in this sentence with your topic sentence.

24. A Mystery Object

Most of us take our surroundings for granted and seldom really see those objects that are part of our everyday lives. We look at these objects, but we don't see them because they have become part of the background. In this assignment, you are asked to focus on an object—nothing unusual, just an everyday object. It will be your writing assignment to describe this object so clearly that anyone reading what you have written will immediately know what you are describing even though you never name the object.

Begin this assignment by looking around for an object to describe. Once you have done that, fill in the information below and then move on to writing your descriptive paragraph.

Mystery Object

Size ______________________

Shape ______________________

Color ______________________

Texture ______________________

Special Features

____

____

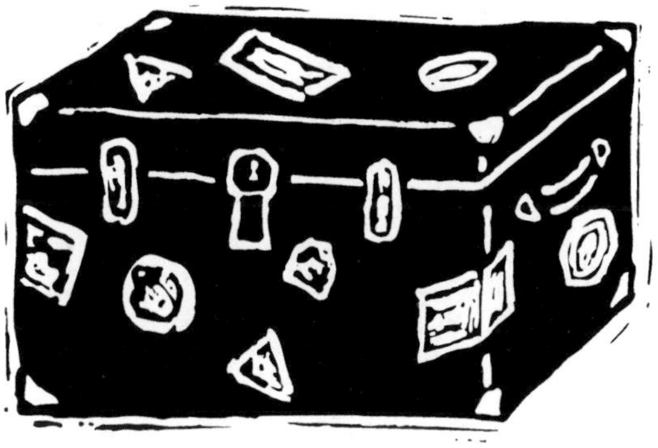

Topic Sentence and Paragraph Pattern

My mystery object is an everyday item that you have looked at dozens of times, even though you may not have seen it.

1. Explain the difference between looking and seeing.
2. Go on to write a full description of your object.
3. Ask your readers if they can identify the mystery object.
4. Finish by commenting on how much people look at and how little they see.

25. A Tree

At first glance, "A Tree" might not seem like much of a topic. If you think about it, however, you can see all kinds of possibilities. For example, did you ever climb a tree to get a better look at the world around you? Or were you lucky enough, when you were younger, to have a tree house in which you and your friends could pretend all kinds of adventures? If not that, how about a special tree that you passed each day on your way to school? If one of these situations matches your experience, you are all set to write a descriptive paragraph or two about a tree.

If none of these situations works for you, there is another way you can approach this topic. To do this, you will need a tree field guide. Look through the field guide and select a tree that sounds interesting to you. You might try researching an elm tree. These trees shaded the streets of many New England towns until the Dutch elm disease began its relentless attack on elms. If not elms, how about pine trees? In the early days of the United States, thousands of these trees were felled and sent back to England. Once there, they were used to build the masts for England's great navy. If neither of these trees is of interest, look up the horse chestnut tree or the willow tree or any tree that strikes your fancy. Look at a picture of the tree. With the help of the picture and the help of the information the tree guide supplies, write a descriptive piece about the tree.

Topic Sentence and Paragraph Pattern

Just like people, some trees are special.

1. Write a sentence in which you identify the tree you wish to write about, and describe where it can be found. Use a descriptive word to describe the tree. For example, you might say a "graceful" elm tree.

2. In your second sentence tell the reader something about the height of the tree in relationship to other trees around it. Mention the bark of the tree. Is it rough, smooth, slippery, or papery?

3. Briefly describe the shape of the tree's leaves.

4. If you are writing about a specific tree, go on to describe why you selected it. If you are just describing a type of tree, continue by explaining why you selected this species.

5. Finish up by writing a summarizing statement about the tree. If you have never seen one of this species, you might comment on where you would have to go to see a tree of this kind. If the tree you are writing about has special meaning for you, you might want to mention that one more time.

26. Observation I

Often in school or at work you will be asked to describe something you have seen. It is important under these circumstances to be accurate and logical in your description. In order to arrange what you have seen in a logical manner, develop a plan: Are you going to describe the scene from left to right? top to bottom? close up to far away, or far away to close up?

Below you will find a detailed drawing. It is your assignment to describe this drawing to someone. Since there isn't any color in this drawing, you must rely on describing the location, size, and appearance of those objects in the drawing that you think the other person should know about. Study the drawing carefully, and then go on to the topic sentence and paragraph pattern.

Topic Sentence and Paragraph Pattern

The drawing is of an outdoor scene.

1. In your next sentence, name, describe, and indicate the location of a specific object in the drawing. You might begin with the lake, which is at the left in the drawing.

2. Continue by describing what is between the lake and the cabin.

3. Go on to give details about the cabin. You might mention the porch on the front of the structure. You could also include information about the doors and windows and even the chimney.

4. Describe the trees that shade the cabin. Indicate their location in relationship to the cabin.

5. In your last sentence, describe your reaction to the scene. For example, "It looks like a wonderful place to spend a peaceful day."

27. Observation II

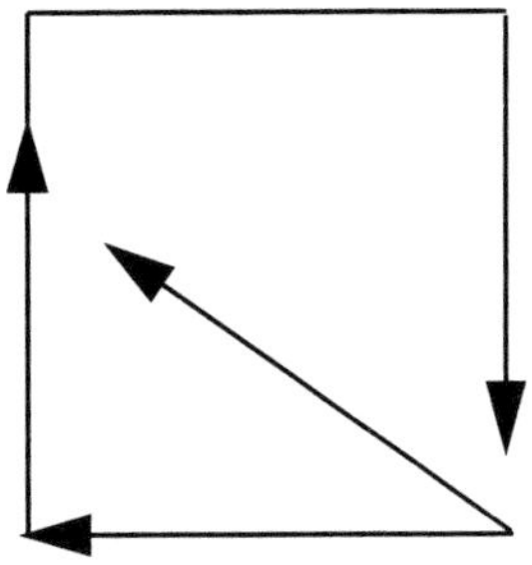

If you have not done so, you should complete Lesson 26 before moving on to this writing assignment. In Lesson 26 your task was to write a description of a drawing. You were advised to arrange your description in such a way that the reader could envision the total picture. In this assignment, you are asked to select your own scene to describe.

You might describe a classroom scene, a cafeteria scene, a scene on a bus, on the street, or even on television. What is important is to select a scene that will require you to guide your reader through the elements of the scene as you did the drawing in Lesson 26. You may decide to describe the scene from right to left, left to right, top to bottom, bottom to top. Whatever you decide to do, stick with your plan.

Words called *transitional words* can help you guide your reader through your writing. *Transitional words* transport (move) your reader from one sentence to another. Notice the transitional word that moves the reader from sentence one to sentence two in the following:

> "We saw a small lake before us. Beyond it lay the mountain we had come to see."

Notice that the word *beyond* shows the reader the relationship between the mountain and the lake. Other transitional words are *nearby, farther, later, in addition, next, after,* and many similar ones. As you write your observation, keep in mind that it is your responsibility to guide your reader through your writing. When you prepare your final copy of this assignment, be sure that you have supplied enough transitional words to move your reader from sentence to sentence easily.

Topic Sentence and Paragraph Pattern

As I looked at the scene before me, I realized it would take some time for me to understand exactly what was happening.

1. Begin your next sentence by selecting this first thing you want to describe. You might begin with "Right in front of me I saw . . . ."

2. Now, decide if you are going to move your eye and your sentence to the rear of the scene or to the left or right. Make your decision and write your sentence. You could begin your sentence with "Nearby I saw . . . ."

3. Continue by identifying and describing the other elements of the scene. Be sure that your reader can picture what you are describing.

4. Finish your paragraph by returning to the idea you expressed in the first sentence. You might want to begin with a sentence like "Careful observation had proved . . ." and then go on to explain what your observation proved.

28. Comfort Foods

In previous assignments, you have written about comfort foods in general, told a story about comfort foods, and written a persuasive paragraph on a comfort food you feel others should include in their diets. In this assignment, you are asked to describe your dream meal. What foods would you bring together at one time if you could select anything you wanted? This meal would be the comfort meal to end all comfort meals.

Since the purpose of this writing is to include descriptive detail, be sure that you not only name the foods you would include in your dream meal but also describe them. You might want to extend this piece by including the recipe for one of the dishes you name. If you have friends who are completing this assignment, too, you could put together a cookbook of your favorite recipes.

Topic Sentence and Paragraph Pattern

*If I could choose a dream meal I would choose*____________________.

1. Describe the different dishes that would make up your meal, using adjectives that appeal to the reader's senses of taste, smell, sight, and sound. Some suggestions are *sizzling, fragrant, moist, gooey, lemony, crisp, bubbling, sweet,* and *chewy*. You can think of lots more.

2. If you are going to enjoy a dream meal, why not enjoy it in a perfect environment? Where would you consume this dream meal? in a large, fashionable restaurant? by the ocean? at a diner? in your own home? Explain to your reader why you would select this location.

3. Continue your essay by naming the people you would invite to enjoy this meal with you. If possible, explain why you would choose each.

4. Finish by making a statement about the dream meal.

____

____

____

____

Editing Practice IV

Read the following essay and suggest ways in which the writer could improve this piece. As in previous revising and editing assignments, read the directions the student received very carefully to be sure the work was completed as assigned. Then move on to consider topic sentences and supporting details. Since this was to be a descriptive piece, be sure the writer has included descriptive words and details which help readers to experience vicariously what the writer is describing.

Student Assignment

Write about your least favorite meal. Remember that your reader needs to see, smell, taste, and dislike this meal as much as you do. Include details that explain why you are sometimes expected to eat this meal. Go on to explain how this makes you feel. Finish the paragraph by restating the idea expressed in the topic sentence of the essay.

Student Paper

Pickled Pigs' Feet

Line 1 One of the foods I dislike the most is pickled pigs'
Line 2 feet. My father loves these things so much that my mom
Line 3 buys them for him as a special treat. When she brings
Line 4 them home from the grocery store I no that they are going
Line 5 to appear on the dinner table at night and I am going to
Line 6 be expected to eat them. Mom always puts the pigs' feet
Line 7 in a plate which makes them look even more disgusting
Line 8 than they already are. According to my farther, his
Line 9 family ate pickled pigs' feet with mashed potatos and
Line 10 green beans. Maybe his family enjoyed this mixture but I
Line 11 can't imagine any one liking them.
Line 12 I don't think Mom likes them very well, but she
Line 13 manages to eat them without saying anything but I can't

Line 14 do that. Its ok with me if my father wants to eat pigs' feet

Line 15 but I don't understand why I have to force them down.

Line 16 Pickled pigs' feet will never be served in my home when I

Line 17 grow up.

Putting It Together

If you have followed the lessons in this book in sequence, you have now written four pieces about comfort foods. You have written in an informative manner by collecting information, narratively by telling a story about comfort foods, persuasively by addressing the pros and cons of a particular food, and descriptively by writing a detailed description of a meal.

In this last writing assignment, you are asked to read over what you have written on comfort foods and decide how you could best put the four pieces together to produce an essay on comfort food. You should find that the different pieces will flow together quite smoothly.

You will need to add a final paragraph if the essay is to reach any kind of conclusion. A topic sentence and paragraph pattern follow for you to consider.

Topic Sentence and Paragraph Pattern

Comfort foods are important for a variety of reasons.

1. Refer back to your first comfort food paragraph and mention that most people have a comfort food.
2. Go on to explain that foods become part of traditions and memorable events.
3. Continue to write about the benefits of comfort foods that are selected for good health.
4. Explain how satisfying it is to look at a special meal.
5. Finish the piece by writing a sentence which sums up your attitude towards comfort foods.

Remember to follow your two-step editing process before rewriting this essay in final draft form.

Key to Editing Practices

I. Orville Wright

Page 21

You should notice that the piece is entitled "Orville Wright" but gives more information about Wilbur than it does Orville. You should also notice that the writer did not include a topic sentence explaining why Orville was chosen as the subject of this paragraph.

Grammatical Errors and Spelling Errors

1. Line 1, comma after *1850*
2. Line 2, *then* should be *than*
3. Line 2, *there* should be *their*
4. Line 2, comma after *father*
5. Line 4, *interestd* should be *interested*
6. Line 6, *the* should be *The*
7. Line 6, comma after *newspaper*
8. Line 7, *West Side News* should be in italics
9. Line 7, comma after *News*
10. Line 7, *Its* should be *It*'s
11. Line 9, comma after *Finally*
12. Line 9, comma after 1903
13. Line 10, *there* should be *their*
14. Line 10, *Flyer* should be in italics

II. *Neighbors*

Page 40

As in the first revising and editing practice, the student who wrote this piece forgot to follow the instructions, which clearly say "Begin your writing with a topic sentence that tells your reader why you are telling the story." The ending of the story is too abrupt, and that the lack of a good topic sentence makes it difficult to end the piece smoothly.

You should also notice the writer's overuse of the word "and"—in lines 2, 5, 6, and 8. On the plus side, notice that the piece is arranged in chronological order, as the instructions directed. Also notice that the story is told clearly. There is no confusion as to what happened.

Grammatical Errors and Spelling Errors

1. Line 2, comma after *remember*
2. Line 4, comma after *yard*
3. Line 5, period after *them,* remove *and*
4. Line 7, *Harris* should be *Harris'* or *Harris's*
5. Line 7, period after *yard*
6. Line 8, remove *and Charlie said*
7. Line 9, quotation mark after the period
8. Line 8, period after *it* should be comma
9. Line 12, *Georges surprise* should read *George's surprise*
10. Line 9, "(close quotation marks) at end of sentence

11. Line 10, comma after *fence*

12. Line 12, *Marias* should be *Maria's*

13. Line 12, *Harris* should be *Harris'* or *Harris's*

14. Line 17, *its* should be *it's*

15. Line 18, *Your* should be *You're*

16. Line 20, *Mrs. Harris'* is correct but could also be *Mrs. Harris's*

17. Line 21, *there* should be *their*

III. If Latin Isn't Dead, It Must Be Alive *Page 61*

Notice this essay's strong opening. By quoting a rhyme, the writer gets the reader's attention. Also notice that the thesis statement ("Latin is alive and well") makes it clear that the writer is going to support that statement.

As you read through the essay, note that the writer has offered a con in the paragraph which begins "The obvious response" and has responded to that con. In the next two paragraphs, the writer supports the topic sentence. The last paragraph returns to the thesis. This is a well-organized and well-written persuasive essay.

Grammatical Errors and Spelling Errors

1. Line 1, *latin* should be capitalized

2. Line 4, *romans* should be capitalized

3. Line 6, *its* should be *it's*

4. Line 13, *latin* should be capitalized

5. Line 14, *know* should become *known*

6. Line 14, *everyday* should be *every day*

7. Line 18, *documents* should not be capitalized

8. Line 19, *then* should be *than*

9. Line 27, *english* should be capitalized

IV. Pickled Pigs' Feet *Page 81*

This assignment offers you an opportunity to add descriptive detail. The writer has made it clear that pickled pigs' feet disgust her but has failed to explain why. You should see that this essay is quite strong as it stands. All that it needs is descriptive words.

Corrections

1. Line 4, comma after *store*

2. Line 4, *no* should be *know*

3. Line 5, *that* needed after *and*

4. Line 7, comma after *plate*

5. Line 8, *farther* should be *father*

6. Line 9, *potatos* should be *potatoes*

7. Line 10, comma before *but*

8. Line 11, *any one* should be *anyone*

9. Line 12, *them* should be *pigs' feet*

10. Line 13, comma after *anything*

11. Line 14, *its* should be *it's*

12. Line 14, *ok* should be *OK*

13. Line 14, comma needed after *pigs' feet*